You Don't Just Drink It!

What you need to know

— and do —

before drinking mead

Beatrice Walditch

You Don't Just Drink It!
What you need to know – and do – before drinking mead
Beatrice Walditch

Cover illustration by David Taylor

ISBN 978-1-905646-24-1

Published by

Heart of Albion
113 High Street, Avebury
Marlborough, SN8 1RF

albion@indigogroup.co.uk

Visit our Web site: www.hoap.co.uk

Printed in England by Booksprint

Contents

What is mead?   1
A toast to the ancestors   2
What's in a name?   7
Wassail!   9
Mead in all its varieties   12
A gift from the gods   16
Mead and the Scandinavian World Tree   18
The mead hall   22
Taliesin's Song of Mead   24
Mead and Druids   26
The Red Drink of Irish sovereignty   28
Mead of inspiration   30
St Bartholomew and the Worshipful
        Company of Mead Makers   31
Mead in the White House   32
How to drink mead   33
Who to honour with the mead   41
Checklist for mead drinking rituals   44
How to make mead   45
Measurements and nomenclature   46
Homebrew equipment   47
Preparation for brewing   48
Basic mead recipe   49
Starting brewing   49
The all-important notebook   52
Bottling   53
Labelling the bottles   55
Mead 'champagne'   57
Basic metheglin recipe   59
Basic cyser recipe   60
Basic pyment recipe   61
Basic omphacomel recipe   62

Other omphacomel recipes   63
'Omphacomel champagne' recipe   64
Basic melomel recipe   65
Basic mead-with-grain recipe   67
Honeyjack   69
Other mead recipes   70
The last drops   71
Sources   72

What is mead?

In recent years the word 'mead' has come to mean an alcoholic beverage brewed from honey and water. The alcohol content ranges from about eight to eighteen percent alcohol by volume (ABV). It may be dry, semi-sweet or sweet. Commercial varieties are usually still but homebrewed versions may be naturally sparkling – 'mead champagne'.

As I will explain, mead is the oldest-known alcoholic drink and familiar to a great many traditional societies. Historical recipes for mead usually included grain or fruit with the honey during the fermentation stage. Spices were also added. There are many names for all the different combinations – some of these are described later – but in a sense they are all different types of mead.

The lack of a clear definition of what mead 'really is' unfortunately means that some commercial meads are not brewed from honey but instead made from wine flavoured with honey. If you have tasted some rather sickly concoction which tastes strongly of honey then you have probably been fooled by one of these offerings. If this rather unpleasant-tasting brew is your first taste of mead then understandably you are likely to ignore the real thing when it is available. But that would be a great mistake!

A toast to the ancestors

Each sip of mead you drink means you are maintaining a tradition which goes back at least 9,000 years. So before drinking mead you need to toast the ancestors. But who might those ancestors be?

Archaeologists in northern China have found pottery vessels with traces of mead, rice and various fruits – along with organic compounds which are created by fermentation. And these pots can be dated to around 7,000 BC.

So far there is no direct evidence for prehistoric mead-making in Europe and Britain. But from about 10,000 BC people were growing grain in the area which is now eastern Turkey, Armenia and northern Iran and Iraq. This culture was 'exported' to Europe and reached the British Isles around 3,500 BC or a little later. Mention grain now and we think of bread. But why go to all the effort of grinding the grains into flour when you can boil them in water or milk? With a little honey to sweeten it the result is something between porridge and rice pudding. And if the leftovers are allowed to ferment something even more enjoyable is produced!

Early meads were most likely produced from grain, honey and water. When the prehistoric henge at Avebury was being built between about 3,000 and 2,600 BC then the nearby valleys were full of limes trees as archaeologists have recognised the pollen of the small-leaved lime or *Tilia cordata* in samples of prehistoric soils. As anyone who has lived near lime trees knows, each year they

Part of the Neolithic henge at Avebury, Wiltshire built between 3,000 and 2,500 BCE. The rituals and celebrations here could easily have involved drinking mead.

produce masses of flowers which drip sticky nectar. And this nectar attracts lots of bees. And the bees make this nectar into an attractive-tasting honey.

Before modern mechanised ways to remove honey from honeycombs, the combs were crushed and the honey squeezed out. What was left was a rather messy mixture of beeswax and honey. The beeswax was useful and the honey residue could be washed off with warm water. But there was no way this honey water would be thrown away! This was of course the starting point for mead-making. As will be discussed later traditional meads were made with a variety of grains, fruits or spices rather than purely with honey.

Perhaps the Ethiopian mead, called *tej*, offers some clues. To give is a sharper flavour the powdered leaves and bark

An Ethiopian woman pouring tej *into a* berele.

of gesho – a species of buckthorn – are added. This is very much like adding hops to beer. The Ethiopians also brew a sweeter, less-alcoholic version called *berz*, which does not need to be aged for so long. The traditional vessel for drinking *tej* is a rounded vase-shaped container called a *berele*.

The oldest written reference to mead is in the hymns of the Rigveda which are usually considered to have been composed between 1,700 and 1,100 BC. And the ancient Greeks were said to prefer mead to any other drink. Aristotle, who lived between 384 and 322 BC, must have been fond of this tipple because his treatise on earth sciences called *Meteorologica* includes a discussion of mead. Clearly so much thinking about weather phenomena, earthquakes and such like could cause the mind to wander…

Pliny the Elder, who included mead in his treatise called Naturalis Historia.

Pliny the Elder – who lived between AD 23 and 79 – included a recipe for mead in his tome *Naturalis Historia*. He called it *militites* and was careful to distinguish mead from wine sweetened with honey. Sadly some commercial producers today sell rather sickly honey-sweetened wine as mead.

Pliny's brew required one part of old honey to three parts of 'rainwater kept for several years' or boiled springwater. This should ideally be left in the sun for forty days and then left on a shelf near the fire – although, Pliny tells us, some people left it to ferment for only nine days. He goes on to say 'with age it attains the flavour of wine.'

Romans too enjoyed mead. The naturalist Columella, who lived in Spain, wrote a book called *De Re Rustica* in about AD 60 and also included a recipe.

However mead is not only brewed and drunk in the northern hemisphere. In the south-eastern parts of South Africa a mead known as *Qhilika* is one of the traditional drinks of the Xhosa people. A commercial brand – with curious flavourings such as coffee or chilli – is available from the Makana Meadery based in Grahamstown.

But, as we will discover, mead becomes most closely associated with Scandinavian and Anglo-Saxon cultures.

What's in a name?

The word 'mead' itself also tells us that word – and the drink – have been around for a very long time. The Sanskrit word *madhu* – which has the multiple meanings of 'sweet; sweet drink; wine; honey' – hints at a much older word which also surfaces in the earliest Germanic languages as *meduz*. Later Germanic languages such as Frisian and Dutch have the word *mede* while Old High German has *metu* which is shortened in modern German to *Met*.

Words such as *med* and *medovina* ('mead wine') are found in Czech, Slovak, Serbian, Bosnian, Bulgarian, Macedonian and Croatian. In the Baltic there is *medus*. Polish people refer to honey as *miód* (pronounced 'mju:t') and mead as *miód pitny* while in Russia *medovukha* remained popular. This drink was also called *sbiten* – a word which crops up often in the novels of nineteenth-century Russian writers such as Dostoevsky, Gogol and Tolstoy.

The Greek word for wine is *methy*. The Old Irish language has *mid* while the Welsh speak of *medd* and Bretons of *mez*. But just to confuse things when Chaucer wrote in the fourteenth century about 'meeth' he was referring to the honey-with-spices drink metheglin and not mead made purely from honey.

And the Finns also seem to be confusing things as they call mead – and sweet mead-like drinks – *sima*. This Finnish word shares its origins with the English word zymurgy. Never heard of zymurgy? Then you're not a zymologist! Zymologists are chemists with the interesting job of looking after the chemistry of wine-making and brewing.

The word comes from the Greek, *zyme* meaning 'a leaven' or yeast. It also gives us the word 'enzyme'.

On May Day in Finland a supply of *sima* is essential. Modern recipes usually substitute brown sugar for honey and include the pulp and rind of a lemon. Then raisins are added during the secondary fermentation to control the sweetness. Handily the raisins rise to the top of the bottle when the drink is ready for consumption.

Speaking of mead-related folk customs, according to a great number of websites, 'honeymoon' derives from an old Persian custom of giving the happy couple mead for the first month after the wedding. However don't be taken in by this misinformation! If you really want to know, 'honeymoon' goes back to at least the early sixteenth century and was originally ironic – indicating that the newly-wed's intense 'sweetness' would be as changeable as the moon, which is no sooner full than it begins to wane. The French also speak of *la lune de miel* (literally 'moon of honey') while the German expression *flitterwochen* (literally 'tinsel week') shares the same irony. The sense of honeymoon as a post-wedding holiday is much more recent, starting about 1800.

Wassail!

One custom we can be sure goes back to Anglo-Saxon times is to wish your fellow drinkers 'Wassail!'. More accurately you should be wishing one person *waes hael* or *hael wes thu* (*thu* is the singular of 'you') and a group of people *wesath hale* as these are the actual Old English words used by the Anglo-Saxons. The Old English words mean 'be in good health' but with the wider sense of 'be fortunate in everything you do'.

Somewhen around the twelfth century the Normans took the mickey out of the inhabitants of the Danish-speaking parts of northern England for responding to 'wassail' with 'drink hail'. This has the sense of 'drink in good health' or just 'happy drinking'. The twelfth century historian Geoffrey of Monmouth retells the story of Rowena and included the exchange *wes heil* and *dric heil*. But early printed editions of his work corrupted the spelling. And Geoffrey was just making things up (as he was wont to do) when he claimed this custom dates back to the fifth century – his source for the Rowena story is Nennius who has none of this drinking malarky.

If you really want to show off your erudition then respond to 'wassail' with *sit heill* – 'sit in good health' – as this is the phrase which occurs several times in old Scandinavian sagas.

The word 'wassail' is now especially associated with cider drinking and the noisy folk customs called 'wassailings' which take place during early January in the orchards where apples and pears are grown for cider early January. But the word wassail was once widely used when drinking

*Rob Wilson and friend wassailing the apple trees at
Hunger Hill allotments, Nottingham, 23 January 2005.*

any brewed drink. Although few originals have survived, beautifully carved wooden vessels known as 'wassail bowls' were once more widespread. Such traditional wassail bowls were carved from fine-grained wood such as lime, although in more recent centuries they were emulated in pottery and even metal.

One occasion – perhaps *the* occasion – when Anglo-Saxons would have brought out the wassail bowl and filled it with the finest mead would have been at the midwinter feast. The Venerable Bede, writing at the beginning of the eighth century, tells us this feast was known to the pre-Christian British as 'Mother's Night'. Nothing else is known for certain but the best guess is that this was the night to honour the triple Mother Goddess known to the Romans as Dea Matrae or Dea Matronae and to the Germanic and Scandinavian societies as *disir*. These were the words used to refer collectively to the local 'spirits of place', the *genii loci*, the chthonic goddesses of the land and its fertility. Every farmstead had their own local manifestation of this spirit-deity, just as Scandinavian farms to this day still have an Otherworldly *vordr* who protects the land and its inhabitants.

And, no, it is not simply coincidence that the Virgin Mary became a mother at Christmas. Put two and two together about the ritual use of wooden bowls at this most important of the pre-Christian feasts and it's no surprise that early Church fathers insisted on the chalices used for Mass were made instead from metal…

Mead in all its varieties

I have already mentioned that the ingredients for traditional meads may be more than just honey and water. The possible combinations of fruit, grain and spices are are far too numerous to list here. To complicate things further a specific combination may have more than one name. So a mead made with apples and cinnamon could be called an 'apple metheglin' or a 'cinnamon cyser'.

Mead made with herbs or spices is called a **metheglin** from the Welsh *meddyg* ('healing') and *llyn* ('liquor') – and these *meddygllyns* were indeed originally folk medicines. Traditional metheglins have ingredients such as meadowsweet (*Filipendula ulmaria*, also known as 'mead wort'), hops, cinnamon, cloves, ginger, nutmeg and orange peel – even tea or vanilla. Modern metheglins might include lavender, chamomile or chilli peppers.

However mead does not have to brewed with spices – just as wine can be mulled with spices and warmed just before it is consumed, so too mead can be mulled with spices and various fruits. Served warm it makes an excellent Yuletide drink.

While meads made with grains seem to be rare these days, they were probably once the most typical brews – presumably with meadowsweet (also known as 'mead wort') or other flavourings.

Mead brewed with hops is also known as **braggot** or **brackett,** from the Welsh *bragawd*. Hops were added to wine for medicinal purposes as long ago as Roman times. There is a seventh century recipe which reveals that

Carolingian monks were also adding hops to medicinal brews. But it took until the thirteenth century for German brewers to discover that the sharpness of hops offsets the sweetness of ale and beer brewed from malted grains. However this idea does not seem to have been taken up by British brewers until the seventeenth or eighteenth centuries .

Presumably the making of meads with meadowsweet goes back a very long time, and would have been a typical mead recipe so had no special name. Once hops began to commercially grown then they would have been easier to obtain than meadowsweet so the terms bragawd, braggot and so on were invented to distinguish them from traditional meads.

Quite whether traditional meads normally included grains is unclear, although I suspect this would have been normal. Quite when people had the idea of making mead with *malted* grains is unclear. It is unlikely to before the eighteenth century and may well be quite a recent innovation.

Mead made with fruit is called a **melomel**. Blackberries, blackcurrants, strawberries, raspberries and plums all create distinctive meads. Mead made with mulberries has

its own name, **morat**. Similarly mead made with rose hips is known as **rhodomel**. Bear in mind that the mead also preserves the fruit so, before bottling, canning or refrigeration, then such fruit was not necessarily removed from the brew before serving!

While mead made with apples or pears is strictly a melomel too, in practice such blends are referred to as **cyser**. Similarly mead made with grapes is called a **pyment**. Homebrewed cysers and pyments are usually made from apple juice or grape juice, not the uncrushed fruits.

One variety of pyment popular in medieval times was called **omphacomel.** These used verjuice – the acidic juice made by pressing crab-apples, unripe grapes or any other sour fruit. Modern versions of omphacomel have been made with lemon or sorrel juice. If you like to experiment with home-brewing – and perhaps blending different batches – then it is fun to find the right balance between the sweetness of the honey and the sourness of the verjuice. The best of such brews or blends have interestingly complex flavours.

Many brands of commercial mead are quite sweet – some excessively so! They are best thought of as dessert wines. Indeed some are nothing more than honey-flavoured wines. Dry mead is harder to come across in shops – and sparkling meads are even rarer to buy – but well worth brewing! Meads made for immediate consumption are in some respects similar to ciders and light ales so are often drunk while still effervescent. However champagne-like meads – where the fizz is created by secondary fermentation after bottling – are also possible.

With all the possible options for adding extra ingredients to mead, a name has had to be invented for meads which have no added fruit, spices or other flavourings! These are known as **show meads** because such blends are entered into competitions at homebrew festivals. They are trickier to produce as, without the fruit and such like, yeast nutrients are needed. More information on how to brew mead later!

A gift from the gods

The Scandinavian sagas written down in the thirteen century – but originally composed several centuries before then – often mention mead. It was the appropriate drink to serve to honoured guests at feasts as it was thought of as a gift from the gods, and referred to as the 'mead of poetry', or the 'mead of inspiration' and other such metaphors.

One of the sagas, *Skáldskaparmál,* describes how the two warring groups of gods – the Aesir and the Vanir – concluded a truce by all spitting into the same vessel. From this mixture of salivas the demi-god Kvasir was born. He had some of the wisdom of each god whose spittle he was conceived from. Once he grew up he travelled widely, teaching and spreading his knowledge. It was said that there was no question he could not answer.

But one night he stayed with two spiteful dwarfs, Fjalar and Galar. They were envious of his wisdom and fame. So they killed him and drained his blood into two vats. They knew that if they drank some of this blood they would begin to acquire some of Kvasir's wisdom and skill with words. But they knew too that fresh blood would soon go off, so they mixed it with honey to preserve it. But after a few weeks they found they had brewed the Mead of Poetry.

Now Odinn famously had two ravens – Hugin and Mugin (the names roughly translate as 'thought' and 'memory'). The two birds left Odinn's shoulders each morning and flew in different directions all day before coming back to their perches on either side of the god's head. They whispered to Odinn everything they had seen and heard

The Gotland image stone known as 'Stora Hammars III' depicts Odin in his eagle disguise (not completely effective – spot the eagle's beard), Gunnlöð holding the Mead of Poetry, and Suttungr her father looking on.

that day. So, thanks to the ravens, Odinn was aware that the dwarves had the Mead of Poetry.

At first the two dwarves told the gods that Kvasir had drowned in his own intelligence. And then, according to the sagas, they invited a giant and his wife to visit them. We have no idea why, or why the dwarves then took the giant out to sea in a boat, before capsizing the vessel and letting the giant drown. Understandably when the devious dwarves told the giant's wife of her husband's death she was distraught. They offered to take her to the place where her husband had drowned but as soon as she had crossed the threshold of the dwarves' house, one of them killed her by dropping a millstone on her head.

When Suttungr, the son of the giants, heard of these dreadful deeds he too went to visit the dwarves. He then led them to a sandbank which he knew would be covered with water at high tide. The dwarves implored him to spare their lives and offered him the Mead of Poetry in compensation for his parents' deaths. Suttungr agreed and brought it back home and instructed his daughter, Gunnlöd, to guard it. Because of this the Mead of Poetry is also called the Mead of Suttungr or *Suttungmjaðar*.

Odinn also was nothing if not a devious character. He thought he too could benefit from some of the Mead of Poetry. But rather than approach Suttung directly instead he went off, in disguise under the name Bölverk, to visit Suttung's brother, who was called Baugi.

As Odinn was approaching Baugi's farm he saw nine slaves scything hay. He offered to sharpen their scythes with his whetstone. But this was a magical whetstone. It worked so well that each of the slaves wanted to buy it. Odinn simply threw the whetstone up in the air and then watched as the slaves fought over the stone. One by one they cut each other's throats in the fighting and they all died.

Odinn then went to Baugi's house, introduced himself as Bölverk and asked to stay the night. He asked how things were going and Baugi replied that he was in a very difficult position as all his slaves had been killed and he did not know how he would get the hay crop in quickly enough. And without enough hay his cattle and horses would die over the winter. 'Bölverk' made him an offer. He would get the hay in for Baugi so long as he had a taste of the Mead of Poetry as his reward. 'Bölverk' made a good job of the hay harvest and so he and Baugi went to Suttung to get his reward. Suttung refused. Not even a single drop of the Mead of Poetry would he allow to Bölverk.

More trickery was needed! Bölverk gave Baugi a magical drill and asked him to dig through the mountain between Baugi's farm and Suttung's home. Baugi in turn tries to trick

Odinn on his eight-legged horse called Sleipnir. Is that a mead cup he is holding in his left hand?

Bölverk. But finally there is a hole through the mountain. Bölverk shape-shifts into a snake and slithers into the hole. Baugi tries to hit him with the magical drill but misses.

Bölverk makes his way into Suttung's home and finds Gunnlöd with the mead. He spends three nights with here. Each night he has a draught of mead. But each draught empties a vat.. Once there is no more Mead of Poetry left he transforms himself once again, this time into an eagle, and flies off home.

When Suttung realises the mead has been stolen from him he too takes on the form of an eagle and flies after Odinn (see the Gotland image stone on page 17). He almost succeeds in catching him. The other Aesir see Odinn approaching and place vats so he can spit out the mead. But with Suttung so close behind him he isn't very careful with his aim. So some of the Mead of Poetry sprays backwards. This portion is known as the skald's or rhymester's share (*skáldfífla hlutr*) and when drunk will make them gifted poets.

This is why when a bottle of mead is opened a few drops should be sprinkled over the heads of those present, while saying a toast to the skalds or poets.

Mead and the Scandinavian World Tree

If all this sounds too much like the script for a blood-soaked Hollywood action movie then, predictably, a good story always leads to a remake. Other sagas tell us it is the Vanir god Heimdallr who is said to be the wisest of the gods and able to offer secret knowledge and good counsel. And Heimdallr is especially associated with wisdom-bestowing mead. He becomes supernaturally powerful after drinking *sonar dreyra*. Taken literally this is the 'blood of atonement', meaning the blood from the annual boar sacrifice. However as is often the case in Scandinavian literature, there can easily be some word play going on. What Heimdallr has also drunk is the 'blood of *són*'. And the *són* is one name for the vessel in which the Mead of Poetry is kept. So the 'blood of *són*' is a metaphor for mead.

In the saga *Grimmnismal* there are detailed descriptions of twelve of the gods' dwellings. But mead is drunk in only three – those of the gods Odinn, Heimdallr and Saga. Compared to the other two we know little about Saga except that he is always associated with foresight and prophecy – attributes he shares with Heimdallr and Odinn.

Curiously Heimdallr is also thought of as the World Tree, standing near a lake and reaching up into the skies. The World Tree draws its power from the minerals of the earth. And many sagas recount how at the roots of the World Tree is a spring or well. According to most of the sagas the

A classic depiction of the Scandinavian World Tree first published in FinnMagnusen's Eddalaeren *in 1824.*

water from the well is very pure. A few of the sagas say that it is milk – or at least milky-white water – which flows from the spring. But just a small number get it right. They say that from this spring flows… yes, you've guessed it! Mead. From this Heimdallr gains his wisdom and foresight.

The mead hall

Much less Old English literature survives compared to Scandinavian sagas and, while mead gets plenty of mentions, there is none of the rich mythic symbolism. In Old English poems, such as *Beowulf*, the word 'mead' is almost always found as part of the phrase 'mead hall'. These were single-room buildings up to fifty metres long made of timber with thatched roofs where the lord or king of the local territory lived and held celebratory feasts. If you have seen television documentaries about traditional societies living communally in long houses then this will give some idea of how these might have been. But also imagine a lot of tapestries on the walls and any number of high-status swords, shields, platters and drinking vessels hanging on the walls for display. There would be a hearty fire burning in the centre (chimneys and fireplaces are still in the future!) which would make the hall a pleasantly warm place to be in winter.

The lord would be sat on the 'high seat' with a small number – about six to eight – of his most faithful retainers sharing his table. The implication from the literature is that images of pagan deities may have stood behind or near the lord's high seat. Although he would pay a pagan priest to lead the most important ceremonies, as lord he would be expected to lead all the other rituals – which would most certainly include toasts to the gods and goddesses. We can assume that such rituals would involve the best of the mead – although the lesser warriors seated furthest away from the high seat might only get to drink an ale made only in part from honey.

Above all the mead hall was a place for the lord's warriors to 'bond'. While feasting and drinking there would be entertainment – mostly listening to songs and stories. At certain times of the year the lord would hand out gifts – such as valuable rings or swords – according to merit. Collectively all these pleasures were referred to as 'hall joys'.

These days we may go to a bar or a pub to drink with other people. But from the sixth century in England, Denmark and adjoining areas of southern Scandinavia it was in mead halls where the serious drinking was done. These mead halls evolve into the banqueting halls of more heavily fortified medieval castles. These in turn evolve into more urban banqueting halls of the Tudor era. And these in turn overlap with early 'town halls' which by the nineteenth century are being rebuilt with at least one grand 'ballroom' cum meeting room – the direct descendants of the Dark Age mead halls.

In Scandinavia the oldest name for these halls seems to have been *sal* or *salr* which in Old English become *sele* and *sael*. The word for 'hall' or 'large room' in modern German, Dutch and Swedish is *Saal, zaal* and *zal* respectively. So place-names such as Gamla Uppsala (Sweden) probably refer to such great halls. Indeed the foundations of just such a hall have been found next to the church there – and there are royal graves nearby, confirming that Uppsala was once the centre of a kingdom, and the place where all the religious and celebratory activities took place.

Taliesin's *Song of Mead*

The Mead of Poetry was also known in medieval Welsh literature. The Welsh bard Taliesin, who lived around AD 550, wrote the *Kanu y med* or 'Song of Mead'. This describes legendary sessions of drinking, feasting and boasting by the warriors gathered in the 'mead hall'.

Another medieval Welsh poem attributed (although not very reliably) to Taliesin may also refer to the Mead of Poetry. In the *Song of Amerghain* there are a number of magical pronouncements followed by three questions. This translation is attributed to Lady Gregory:

> I am the wind on the sea
> I am the wave of the sea
> I am the bull of seven battles
> I am the eagle of the rock
> I am the flash from the sun
> I am the most beautiful of plants
> I am a strong wild boar
> I am a salmon in the water
> I am a lake in the plain
> I am the word of knowledge
> I am the head of the spear in battle
> I am the god who puts fire in the head
> Who spreads the light in the gathering on
>   the hills?
> Who can tell the ages of the moon?
> Who can tell the place where the sun sets?

The professional storytelling and shaman Gordon MacLellan has suggested that 'the god who puts fire in the head' is a reference to the effects of drinking mead. And after partaking of the god-gifted Mead of Poetry – the Mead

Llyn Geirionydd, where Taliesin was born after a mythical metamorphosis.

of Inspiration – then the person has the wisdom of a demi-god such as Kvasir and will know the answers to the three questions. Or, as Gordon points out, the person 'has become a living, thinking part of their environment.'

Mead and Druids

Mention Druids and people think of white-robed priests gathering mistletoe with consecrated golden knives before they were annihilated by the Romans when they invaded Britain. And if you know a little about Druids then you may also know that they were accompanied by bards – who wrote poetry and sang songs, as bards are wont to do – and ovates who do what ovates are wont to do – they gave 'ovations'. Which is a polite word for long drawn out speeches involving long lists of kings and other nobles along the lines of who begat who, all the way back to the year dot.

But everything you think you know about Druids has been made up – possibly including their name. Most of what we think about Druids was made up by a bunch of Romantically-inclined antiquarians in the eighteenth century and especially by a somewhat suspect Welsh Nationalist who lived between 1747 and 1826 called Edward Williams writing under the more distinctive moniker of Iolo Morganwg. But by the early twentieth century members of the various Druid orders were a fairly staid bunch with a lot of CofE vicars among their number. But a lot more inspiration has gone into 'making up' Druidry in the last fifty years.

It has to be said that modern day Druids have been responsible for a lot of mead consumption. It is shared at rituals and drunk in more private occasions when seeking inspiration. All the Druids I have ever met (and I've met quite a few over the last fifteen-or-so years) have been

Sharing the mead during a Druidic celebration of summer solstice 2007 at Beacon Hill, Leioestershire.

amiable people with a deep respect for the environment. They often have a detailed knowledge of Welsh medieval literature – the *Mabinogion* and such like. Whether these positive traits were acquired from drinking mead I will leave as an open question...

Later in this book I give details of a ritual which are inspired by various Druidic rituals I have taken part in. We will never know the words and rites which Druids living over two thousand years in the Iron Age may have actually used. But only a little effort is needed to envisage the deep-seated ideas which are likely to have been shared by all people of all eras when embarking on mead drinking rituals.

The Red Drink of Irish sovereignty

Mead does take a leading role in one of the legends retold in medieval Irish literature. The story called *Baile in Scáil* – often referred to in English as *The Phantom's Ecstatic Vision* – describes how King Conn of the Hundred Battles visits an otherworldly house. There he is given food and drink by a woman called either Fldith Erenn or Fldithius Erenn. Her name has the literal meaning of 'noble Ireland' so we should think of her as the sovereign of the land.

She asks 'To whom shall be given this cup with the red drink?' The red drink, *dergflaith* in Irish, is a play on words as the Irish words for 'drink' and 'sovereignty' sound almost the same. After she has serves Conn with the red drink the master of the house – a phantom, no less – enters into a ecstatic trance and foretells the future kings of Ireland.

But there is even more word-play in Irish as *mid*, the word 'mead' is related to the name of Queen Medbh (pronounced 'Maev'). And one of the traditional meanings of Medbh's name is 'the one who intoxicates'. Just as likely her name is a contraction of Gaulish and Indo-European royal names which translate as 'horse sacrificer'. Both meanings fit well with her main role as in legends she is one of the most important female sovereigns of the land while also boasting to her husband, Ailill, of how easily she tempts and seduces young heroes. Or, as she puts it, 'I never had one man without another waiting in his shadow'. Sadly medieval writers didn't go in for writing chick-lit so we don't have *Queen Medbh's Diary* with all the details.

The Scandinavian sagas provide one reason why a sprinkling of mead needs to be offered to the ground. The Irish reveal that perhaps the deeper meaning is that this is the drink of the sovereign queen of the land, so closely related to the Dea Matronae and the *disir*.

But we do not have to go back to ancient literature to read about the importance of mead. Many popular twentieth century writers have picked up on the magic of mead, including J.R.R. Tolkein, George R.R. Martin and Neil Gaiman. My personal favourite is Gaiman's novel *American Gods* published in 2001 as this successfully interweaves his knowledge of the Scandinavian god Odin or Woden with modern day American culture. Gaiman's characters refer to mead as the drink of the gods. But I'll leave it to the likes of Wikipedia-ists and other completists to cite all the references to mead in fantasy fiction.

Mead of inspiration

With all these thoughts of gods and sovereign queens you will now no doubt be feeling the need to write down a few stories of your own. Or do you still need a little more inspiration?

Well, of course the Mead of Poetry is there to help you. As Taliesin put it::

> I am the god who puts fire in the head

But, as you will have gathered by now, you can't just drink it! First you must meet up with local Otherworldly kings and queens, bossy gods and seductive goddesses. Then you must practice all the toasts and libations needed for different eventualities.

Have you stocked up with enough mead to cope ?

One side of the square Anglo-Saxon font at Luppitt, Devon decorated with dragons and a warrior. Possibly the decoration on this font was inspired by smaller wooden vessels used for serving mead.

St Bartholomew and the Worshipful Company of Mead Makers

The patron saint of beekeepers and honey-makers is St Bartholomew. Although one of the twelve apostles he rarely gets mentioned in the Gospels. His feast day is the 24th August and traditionally honey was collected from hives before this day.

Every year the church at Gulval, near Penzance in Cornwall, has a special service of Blessing of the Mead which is attended by members of the Worshipful Company of Mead Makers. The vicar is also the Almoner of the Company. After the service everyone processes to the Mead Hall, where the vicar blesses a loving cup – or 'mazer' – full of mead before this is shared by those taking part.

Mazers for drinking mead were traditionally made of bird's-eye maple with silver rims.

Gulval church as shown on a postcard dated 1903.

Mead in the White House

During the election campaign in August 2012, the White House released details of the recipe for President Barack Obama's home-brewed honey ale. This is believed to be the first-ever beer made at the White House. 'The recipe was kept under wraps until 13,000 people signed an online petition demanding to know it, and someone even filed a freedom of information request,' reported the BBC in early September.

The ingredients included light malt extract, amber crystal malt, honey, gypsum, yeast and corn sugar.

According to Sam Kass, the assistant chef at the White House who has taken on responsibilities for brewing, 'Since our first batch of White House Honey Brown Ale, we've added the Honey Porter and have gone even further to add a Honey Blonde this past summer. Like many home brewers who add secret ingredients to make their beer unique, all of our brews have honey that we tapped from the first ever bee-hive on the South Lawn. The honey gives the beer a rich aroma and a nice finish but it doesn't sweeten it.'

Barack Obama at the Iowa State Fair, August 2012. Photographer unknown.

How to drink mead

I'll try to be brief. Which is more than can be said for the scholar Michael Enright who devoted a whole tome to the significance and rituals associated with serving and drinking mead in the Dark Ages. Track down a copy of his 1996 book, *Lady with a Mead Cup* if you really do want to know everything there is to know and plenty more besides.

Suffice to say that the most honoured role of the wife of the head of the house – the leader of the clan or 'war band' at such festivities – was to take the mead cup around in turn to each of the guests. The trickiest part was to serve everyone in their order of importance to avoid any insults or loss of honour.

But, unless you have a pressing need to entertain a substantial war band, then I'd recommending starting with a group of easy-going friends first. Invite them round for the evening of the full moon. Why the full moon? Well that will become clear later.

With all these libations to be made you really don't want to be doing this in the living room. The dog will get drunk licking up all the droplets from the carpet and as for cats, well they'll just demand mead *every* evening for their supper from now on... And if you've no cats or dogs then the carpet is going to need professional intervention by the morning...

So the back garden it needs to be. If your back garden isn't big enough, or one too many loud 'Wassails' will get attention from nearby neighbours, then you need to go into the local park or woods instead. Yes. The local park at full

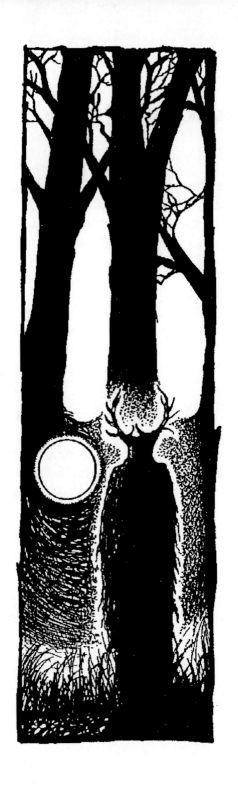

moon. What will people think if they see you? Well, there's an easy answer to that – wear full-length robes with hoods. They'll stop anyone recognising you. And more importantly the local youths who might be up to no good in the park after dark will flee in terror. Remember, they may be younger than you but they've already watched far more horror movies than you ever will. Their imaginations will go into overdrive at the sight of a group of people all in a full set of robes. If you feel the need to provoke abject terror then practice a few X-rated screams while you're in the shower before hand.

If you think a full-length robe isn't frightening enough then borrow a set of stag antlers and tie them on the top of your head. Then everyone will know you're *seriously* pagan. Well, just as long as you don't get a fit of the giggles when the antlers try to fall off...

I digress with a little too much 'inspiration'. It's the mead that does it...

Whatever you think is the right way to go about things, make sure you don't simply unscrew the top and pour some in a glass...

Gather everyone around. Make sure there is someone in each of the four directions – north, south, east and west. This is likely to cause a little consternation because few people these days orientate themselves all the time. To 'orient' originally meant facing east – 'the Orient' – as is the case in traditional churches. People in indigenous cultures tend to know the direction to their home intuitively. Modern people are often not so good – and people who live most of their lives in cities laid out in rectangular blocks usually fare worst of all. Either do some homework before hand so you know which direction is where. But otherwise bear in mind that at the Spring and

Autumn Equinoxes the full moon rises due east. Between the Equinoxes during summer then it will rise further to the north and between the Equinoxes during winter it will rise further to the south. But using a compass to find north is much too much like being in the Scouts – it may be the answer if all else fails but just don't let anyone else see you doing it!

If some people have lanterns which take candles or tealights (don't forget some matches too!) then light four and set them up to mark out the four directions. Battery-operated lights just don't do it though!

Gather everyone round into a circle and join hands. Tell everyone to take a few moments to arrive, to breathe more slowly and deeply than usual for a minute or so, to feel the Earth pushing back at your feet, exactly in balance with your body weight (unless you've found some squidgy mud...). Say something that brings everyone together, like 'We stand here hand to hand and heart to heart.... '.

If you're good at remembering stuff then now's a good time to recite these words from the *Vajur Veda:*

> May there be peace in the heavens, peace in the skies and peace on Earth.
>
> May the waters be plentiful.
>
> May the grasses and herbs bring peace to all creatures,
>
> And may the plants be at peace also.
>
> May the beneficent beings bring us peace,
>
> And may the way of all creation bring peace throughout the world.
>
> May all things be peaceful, and may that peace itself bring further peace.
>
> May we also bring peace to all.

But if you can't remember then please don't read it from a piece of paper – it's so naff. Just call for peace in whatever words come to mind.

There are two options next. One is to loosen hands, and turn to face the east then say 'May there be peace in the east.' Ideally every else repeats this together. Then *turn clockise* (sunwise) to face south and say 'May there be peace in the south', and so forth all the way to the north. Then, if necessary, turn clockwise once more to face back into the middle of the circle. Then say 'May there be peace throughout the world!'. Once everyone has repeated this you can get on with the interesting bit about blessing the mead.

Alternatively, if you think that's not enough ritual, then after the person has recited the call for peace from the *Vajur Veda* (or improvised something similar) everyone else should stay holding hands facing into the circle. The person calling for peace can then simply step towards the east, south, west and north saying 'May there peace in *[whichever quarter]*' and then step to the centre to call for peace everywhere. Ideally everyone else responds with the same words.

After that the circle should turn to face the east and the person who is most easterly say clearly 'We ask the spirits of the east to join our circle! Hail and welcome!' Everyone else then responds 'Hail and welcome!. Step clockwise to the south where the most southerly person calls upon the spirits of the south, ending with the words 'Hail and welcome!'. Continue until all four quarters have been hailed and welcomed then – still turning clockwise if necessary – come to face into the circle again. 'Proper pagans' will come up with quite elaborate calls to the quarters which include the elements air (east), fire (south), water (west) and earth (north). But this is a book about mead not a prescription for changing your life. If you feel a need to go for the whole shebang then you'll need to read a book on pagan rituals too.

Just one thing to remember at this stage. If you do the 'hail and welcome' to the four quarters then at the end of the ritual you need to do a 'hail and farewell' to the four directions too. Details later...

Now make sure everyone is 'together' again then say something along the lines of:

> We call upon the spirits of this place, the spirits of the rocks deep beneath our feet, deposited over millions of years.
>
> We call upon the spirits of the soil of this place, upon which life depends.
>
> We call upon the spirits of the trees and plants of this place – all the trees, all the wild flowers and all the grasses. *[If you're good at botany then a nice variant is to name some of the species of trees, flowers and grasses that grow nearby.]*
>
> We call upon the spirits of the creatures, the birds, the animals and the insects of this place.
>
> We call upon all the spirits of this place to join us today.
>
> Hail and welcome!

To which everyone else responds enthusiastically 'Hail and welcome!'

Now's the moment when you need to remember where you put the bottle of mead. Not always easy in the dark, especially if you put it where no one was likely to step on it (always a good idea). Nestling in the roots of trees is often a good place – but you need to recognise which tree it was by moonlight!

Actually, the best of all is not to go straight to blessing the mead but instead to bless some bread. Nice homemade bread with something tasty in it – I'm found of adding caraway or cumin seeds, but slices of black olives with some dried basil is also an option. If you have a local bakers who produces something special then that would be the easier option. If needs must then the words 'bless this fruit cake' have been heard before now! But mead does go better with bread rather than cake.

So if you're doing the full malarky then at this stage take hold of the bread. Ideally partly-wrap it in a clean cotton napkin or such like – not that I'm usually so fussy. Say something such as:

> We call upon the spirits of the four directions
> to bless this bread.

> We call upon the spirits of this place to bless
> this bread.

> We call upon the sense of deity each of us
> brings to this circle to bless this bread.

The last line can sound a bit clunky but it's usually possible to come up with something suitably embracing that doesn't mean going through a whole encyclopedia's worth of deities.

Break a small piece of bread off for yourself, then pass to the most honoured person in the circle saying 'May you never hunger.' Although a response is not essential, 'So may it be' is appropriate. That person takes a piece of bread and passes it to their left, so the bread moves clockwise. They too offer it saying 'May you never hunger.'

Once the bread has been round once then it's OK to drop the 'May you never hunger' wishes and simply ask 'More bread?' or such like!

Once the bread has started in its travels then it's time to bless the mead. Yes, I know, you thought I'd never get there! Well if you've skipped on the bread then you're here already.

Blessing the mead will come easily if you've just practised by blessing the bread. If not then unscrew the top (or uncork it if it's homebrew – you did remember to bring a corkscrew didn't you?) and say something such as:

>We call upon the spirits of the four directions
>to bless this mead.

>We call upon the spirits of this place to bless
>this mead.

>We call upon the sense of deity each of us
>brings to this circle to bless this mead.

But stop before you hand it to the waiting circle. You can't just drink it! First of all you need to honour those who need honouring.

Who to honour with the mead

Had you realised before that to make one pound of honey bees need to fly about 55,000 miles. That's more than twice the circumference of the earth. That's getting on for 20,000 bee-miles for a 75 centilitre bottle of dry mead.

So the first honouring should always be to the bees!

> We thank the bees for all their industrious work.

Sprinkle a few drops on the ground near the centre of the circle and say 'Know that you are honoured here!' Everyone else responds with 'Know that you are honoured here!'

Then say 'We honour the spirits of this place, of the rock, the soil, the plants and the creatures.' Sprinkle a few more drops and say 'Know that you are honoured here!' then let everyone else respond.

Then – and for me this is the most important of the 'honourings' – say:

> We honour the spirits of our ancestors.
>
> We honour our ancestors of blood from our mothers to their mothers back to all our mothers.
>
> We honour our ancestors of bone from our fathers to their fathers back to all our fathers.
>
> We honour too our ancestors of tribe, and those from whom we have learnt, and from whom we have received guidance.

Another sprinkling and a heartfelt response from everyone 'Know that you are honoured here too.'

If you or members of your group have 'bardic' inclinations or aspirations then this is the right time for the skald'?s or rhymester's share to be sprinkled over those who wish to become gifted poets while honouring the poets of times past.

Now pour the mead (if you've not been too generous with the sprinklings then there should be some left...) into a suitable vessel, take a swig, then offer to the person you gave the bread to and say 'May you never thirst.' They can, if they wish, respond 'So may it be' before taking a sip. They then pass to their left with the words 'May you never thirst.'

There's a variant of this in which an 'honoured woman' – who can either be honoured because of her age or social standing or because of her youth and beauty – takes the mead cup around to each person, offering it to them with the words 'May you never thirst'. This is the better option for groups who may be a bit iffy about sharing the same vessel – the bearer of the cup can discretely wipe the rim with a paper napkin after each sip. If you want to go the 'full mile' with this then prepare in advance a garland of fresh flowers and leaves for this honoured woman to wear in her hair or around her shoulders.

Then rejoin the circle a few people ahead of where the mead is now (you don't want to be thought too keen…) so get a second portion of mead!

With any luck the mead will make it at least once around the circle before running out. This is why you need to do the ritual at the full moon. Because you need to see who's drinking more than their fair share…

But it's always a good idea to have a 'back up' bottle handy!

Once the mead has been around at least once and the mead of inspiration starts to flow then encourage anyone who can sing or tell a good story to contribute. But, before people start to leave, remember to finish with a final joining of hands.

Starting in the north say 'We thank the spirits of the north for joining our celebration tonight. Hail and farewell!' The response is, of course, 'Hail and farewell.' Then turn *anticlockwise* (that's sure to fool some of the folk!) to the west and repeat almost the same words. Then turn again to the south and finally the east.

Then get everyone to join with the parting wish of 'Merry meet, merry part and merry meet again!'

Checklist for mead drinking rituals

So, things to remember to take for mead drinking rituals:

- One or more bottles of mead
- a corkscrew (if the bottles are corked)
- Something suitably ceremonial to drink the mead from (swigging from the neck of the bottle is just *so* heathen...)
- nice bread
- a clean cotton napkin to hold the bread
- possibly a second napkin to wipe the mead vessel
- lanterns with tea lights
- matches

Optional:

- full-length hooded robes
- a stag-antlered head-dress
- a garland of fresh flowers and leaves to put on the head of the person serving the mead

How to make mead

If you've ever had a go at homemade wine then you're well on the way to making mead – and all the many variants. The main drawback to meadmaking is that good honey is usually expensive. Cheaper honeys are acceptable for mixing with strongly-flavoured fruits but dry meads need to be made with a honey which has a distinctive taste. Avoid commercially-blended honeys and use 'monoflora' honeys from heather or clover if you can afford them. If you know a local beekeeper then often their honey will be as good as 'monoflora' ones.

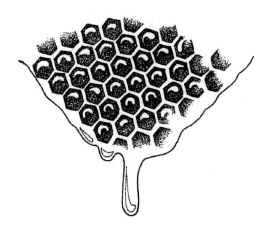

Measurements and nomenclature

The recipes used here work out to nice 'round' numbers of UK gallons and pounds. However it is easy to convert to either US gallons or to litres and kilograms if that is what you are used to.

Similarly I will refer to demijohns. You may know them as carboys. They're the same thing... It is important to check the volume of the demijohn/carboy you use for brewing *before* you start weighing out the honey and other ingredients. If you use demijohns larger than one gallon then be you'll be buying a lot of honey. Which is great if the batch turns out wonderful. But not so good if it needs blending with the same amount of a different batch! Until you get good at meadmaking and can reliably produce good batches then I strongly recommend using one gallon demijohns.

Helpful conversions

> 1 pound = 454 grams
> 1 kilogram = 2.2 lbs (approx. 1 lb 3 oz)
> 1 UK gallon = 1.2 US gallon = 4.55 litres
> 1 US gallon = 16 cups = 128 US fluid ounces
>   = 0.83 UK gallon = 3.79 litres

Homebrew equipment

- several one gallon demijohns/carboys
- one air lock per demijock
- bungs to fit airlocks into necks of demijohns
- large bottlebrush with a handle long enough to easily reach the bottom of a demijohn
- funnel. (If you plan to make melomels then you need a funnel with a neck narrow enough to fit the demijohn but big enough to let crushed fruit through easily.)
- electric heaters to keep demijohns warm (not needed if you have a suitable airing cupboard or similar warm, draught-free place)
- syphon and tubing
- Campden tablets
- wine bottles
- corks
- gadget for putting corks in winebottles
- recycled PET carbonated drinks bottles
- yeast – either brands sold for white wine or champagne or ones sold for meadmaking
- yeast nutrient
- large saucepan
- labels for bottles
- notebook to keep details of batches

Online suppliers will have all these and much more.

Preparation for brewing

All these recipes are for a standard one-gallon demijohn. You'll need an air lock and a suitable sized bottlebrush to clean out the demijohn. Get the inside spotlessly clean then fill with warm water and a couple of Campden tablets (potassium or sodium metabisulfite) crushed between two teaspoons. If you can't get Campden tablets then the sterilising liquid used for babies' feeding bottles ('Miltons' and other brands) will do nicely although this costs more. Either way allow to soak for up to an hour then rinse out with clean water. Pour the sterilising water into a saucepan or something big enough to soak the air lock in. Allow the air lock to soak while you're filling up the demijohn. Remember to keep the sterilising solution as you'll need enough to fill the air lock after it's fitted into the demijohn.

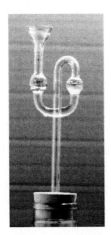

Three types of air lock. The glass ones (left) *break too easily. The cheap plastic ones* (middle) *work but can't be cleaned so a new one is needed for each brew. However the plastic ones on the right work really well!*

Basic mead recipe

The basic recipe for one UK gallon (4.55 litres) of dry mead is:

> 2½ pounds (1.13 kg) of honey
> 1 sachet white wine yeast
> 1 teaspoon yeast nutrient

For one US gallon (3.79 litres) the amount of honey should be reduced to 2 pounds.

Any white wine yeast will do but varieties sold as 'champagne yeast' work best of all as they have the least taste afterwards. I am aware that some brands of yeast are sold just for mead-making – but I've yet to try them!

Because there is no fruit in this recipe then some sort of yeast nutrient is essential. This can be bought in packets and a teaspoonful tipped in. However a couple of vitamin C tablets crushed between two teaspoons work just as well. But to be honest just about every mead brew I've ever made simply included the juice of a large orange. This adds all the nutrients needed but isn't enough to give an orangey taste to the brew. The one time I didn't have any oranges I peeled and crushed two ripe kiwi fruit instead, as these are also very rich in vitamin C.

Even if you prefer your mead 'off-dry' or somewhat sweet I strongly recommend you start by brewing a dry mead. It is always possible to add a little more honey later, whereas a batch which stops fermenting before all the sugars are converted into alcohol will simply stay sweet (although, as I will discuss later, there are some useful ways of blending unwanted sweet batches to get 'champagne mead').

Starting brewing

Some meadmakers favour heating the honey up to boiling point then allowing to cool. This kills off any bugs. But it also spoils the flavour of the honey. I've never boiled any honey – and never had a batch go off or taste 'musty' as a result. But all the honey I've used has been clean. If you're a beekeeper using up 'odds and sods' from centrifuging the combs and putting into jars (and meadmaking is an excellent way of using up such spills and any other honey that might otherwise be wasted) then you may need to boil any honey that may have come into contact with wild yeasts otherwise these will add a strong 'taint' to the brew.

As honey tends to be a bit too stiff to pour into the neck of a demijohn I simply take a large saucepan, put a couple of pints or so of water in and start to warm this up on the stove. Take the top off two one-pound jars of honey and place them, on their sides, in the saucepan. Spoon out half the honey from another jar into the water. Keep an eye on the saucepan, use a spoon to wiggle the two glass jars about so all the honey runs out and then stir the honey into the water. Remove from the heat as soon as the honey has dissolved and remove the empty honey jars.

Add enough clean cold water to bring them temperature down to lukewarm and, using a funnel, pour into the demijohn. Add the yeast and yeast nutrient then enough lukewarm water to fill the demijohn to the shoulder (not to the neck!). Without trying to make an exact science of it, aim to have the liquid in the bottle ending up between 25 and 30C (75^0 to 85^0 F).

Put the air lock and bung firmly in the neck of the demijohn then pour sufficient of the sterilising water into the air lock to 'seal' it. Place the demijohn somewhere warm and away from draughts – in the airing cupboard at the side of the hot water cylinder or next to (but not on top of) an electric storage heater. If, like me, you like in a house with none of these options then frankly you need to invest in one of the special electric heaters made to wrap around demijohns. Place it towards the bottom of the bottle.

This should bubble away nicely for two to four weeks. Once the bubbling has almost stopped then remove the electric heater (if used). Use a syphon (sterilise it well first!) to remove a small sample of the liquid, avoiding any of the must at the bottle. Take a sip. It will still taste too yeasty and have a bit of 'fizz' to it. But, with a bit of practice, you'll get used to checking whether this needs more honey. If you think it could do with just a little more sweetness then dissolve a *dessertspoon* of honey in a little warm water and funnel into the demijohn. Leave to brew for another week.

Don't be tempted to add more than one dessertspoon of honey at a time otherwise you may end up with something far too sweet.

Taste again after a week and, just maybe, add another dessertspoon of honey and leave for another week.

Once you are happy that it's sweet enough then fill up the demijohn to the neck with clean water. Allow to slowly bubble for a few more weeks. Taste again – it should be ready for bottling.

The all-important notebook

Keep a record of the ingredients used in each batch and give the batch a number and date brewing started. And it really does help to know which recipes worked best (and also to know which ones you don't want to repeat!).

Give each demijohn its own batch number. Even if you are making more than one demijohn of the same recipe still use a different batch number for each one as you may 'tweak' each demijohn differently later on. Use a felt-tip pen to mark the batch number on the demijohn. You may think you'll remember which was which but, believe me, you won't!

Batch number: 28
Brew started: 2nd Oct 2011

2½ lbs Norman's honey
1 sachet white wine yeast
1 tspn yeast nutrient

Almost stopped bubbling
17th Nov 2011

Bottled 2 Feb 2012

Bottling

You will need the special gadget for putting corks in wine bottles and a rubber or wooden mallet.

Soak the bottles and corks in hot sterilising liquid for at least thirty minutes – reject any bottles which have even the slightest amount of residue in the bottom.

Also sterilise the syphon. You'll need this to avoid getting any of the must at the bottom of the demijohn into the bottles. Simply trying to pour from the demijohn into a bottle will disturb this must and you'll end up with musty-tasting mead. Not nice!

Some books on winemaking insist on adding Campden tablets to the demijohn just prior to bottling to kill of the yeasts. Personally I dislike the sulphur taste that this gives to the brew – although it is a taste which dissipates the longer the wine is kept in the bottle. But mead has more subtle flavours than wine and is often drunk younger so the sulphites are more intrusive. More importantly, killing the yeast in this way stops any secondary fermentation needed for 'champagne' type meads so *never* use Campden tablets before bottling if you want an effervescent or 'champagne' brew.

So long as everything used at the bottling stage – the syphon, wine bottles and corks – are clean and properly sterilised then there is little risk of a batch going wrong if you don't use Campden tablets. Although when I started winemaking I followed the rule book by using Campden tablets but by the time I started meadmaking I'd stopped using them. I've never had a bottle go 'off' yet!

Bang in the corks, wash any spillage off the bottles then label the bottles with the batch number and the date of bottling.

Frankly I find it much easier to reuse screw-top wine bottles than use traditional corks – although I accept that a bottle with a proper cork does make a better gift.   For 'champagne type meads I always reuse screw-top fizzy drinks bottles (look for the letters 'PET' on the bottom - never use ones which say PVC as they will burst under the pressure). Conventional wine bottles with corks or screw caps are unsuitable for 'fizzy' varieties of mead as the straight corks will simply pop out as the pressure builds up. Screw caps may stay on – but the bottles themselves are not designed to take pressure so may explode violently if knocked. And those shards could go anywhere – including someone's face and eyes.

You really do need to keep dry meads for at least six months and preferably about a year after bottling. 'Champagne' meads can usually be drunk after a couple of months or so.

Mead in naked bottles...
You'll never remember which
batch was which in a few month's
time!

Labelling the bottles

Just as we judge a person by first impressions, or a book by its cover, so too the label on a bottle of wine sets certain 'expectations'. If the label looks a bit tatty or downmarket then we'll expect it to taste no better than a *vin de pays*. Whereas a bottle of Nuits-Saint-Georges is likely to look subtly impressive.

So in the same way you need your mead to give off the right 'first impressions'. If you've got neat handwriting or, better still, some skills with calligraphy then by all means do some stylish hand-written labels for the bottles. Come up with a suitably quirky 'brand name' rather than simply call it 'Mead'. And, for reasons that I will explain next, use waterproof 'Indian' ink and not just felt-tip pens or other pigments which might run if they get damp.

If, like me, handwriting was never your best talent, then computers can readily come to your aid. On the following page are some examples of labels. Use these as inspiration for designing your own in any picture-editing software. Labels printed using inkjet printers are rarely sufficiently waterproof. Bottles are often left to mature in places which are cool enough to attract condensation. And any spills will soak the labels on otherwise undamaged bottles. So if you have a laser printer use that instead, even if it means the label is in black and white rather than colour (although colour lasers are fine if you have one).

But, whether hand-written or computer-aided, remember to add the batch number and the date of bottling in small but clear lettering.

Examples of labels. Don't forget the all-important batch number!

Office suppliers sell sticky-backed labels for both inkjet and laser printers. But unless you plan to write all your labels by hand, don't be tempted to buy the ones with six or eight to the sheet – it simply means that you will get frustrated trying to get the computer to print in the right place! Instead by the one-label-per-sheet variety. Print six labels onto the sheet and cut them up with scissors. Even better, if you have a rotary guillotine, use that so that everything is neat and square.

Mead 'champagne'

Now you've got the hang of the basics let's look at the various variants of mead. First up is 'mead champagne'.

Use only two pounds of honey to a UK gallon, plus yeast and some sort of yeast nutrient but otherwise as the basic dry mead instructions. Save up empty plastic bottles which were sold with carbonated drinks in them. They will probably have the letters 'PET' moulded into the bottom. Do not use bottles which say 'PVC' as these are not suitable for fizzy drinks. You need enough PET bottles to take four litres.

When the demijohns stop bubbling after a few weeks clean out the PET bottles thoroughly and then sterilise them – and the caps – in warm water (not too hot or the bottles will distort!).

Dissolve two or three dessertspoons of honey in warm water. Stir so the honey is fully dissolved. Add an equal amount of this water to each of the PET bottles. If the bottles are different sizes then adjust so there will be the same proportion of honey after the bottles are filled. Fill each bottle *almost* full and put the original cap back on. Keep somewhere warm for the first two or three weeks and then somewhere fairly cool for a few more weeks. Actually it is best if kept for a few months. So I am told... A good batch is just so 'wow' that it doesn't last a few months! Preferably chill in the fridge before serving.

If you end up with a batch of mead which is too sweet – and it may happen – then keep this in its demijohn somewhere fairly cool. Just make sure the air lock never dries out. In the meantime brew up another demijohn with no more than two pounds of honey. When this has more or less stopped bubbling then syphon the overly-sweet batch into PET bottles. But only *half* fill them. Then fill the bottles with the very dry batch. Bear in mind you will need enough PET bottles to take about eight litres of mead! Label these bottles and keep them at room temperature. After a few weeks the secondary fermentation should have started and you're well on the way to having enough mead champagne to get at least a dozen people well on the way to being legless before they've realised how potent this is!

One word of warning. If you intend to take mead champagne on a picnic then do keep it in a cool box. Opening a bottle once it has got warm is likely to mean that half the bottle just squirts everywhere as it is opened – not only a waste of good mead champagne but a very sticky experience for the person who opens it (and their clothes).

I have to admit that of all the varieties of homebrewed mead in these recipes, it is dry mead champagne that is my favourite – closely followed by fizzy mead lemonade, otherwise known as omphacomel champagne.

Basic metheglin recipe

Any mead made with herbs or spices is called a metheglin. Traditional options include meadowsweet (or 'mead wort'), hops, cinnamon, cloves, ginger, nutmeg and orange peel.

The recipe is the same as basic mead. If you're using orange juice as the yeast nutrient then finely chop the peel and add that, together with a teaspoon of cinnamon and *either* cloves or nutmeg (but not both!).

I think adding vanilla, tea or chilli is more of a joke than a 'serious' mead. As such I would not make these from honey-only recipes but instead base them on a mixture of grain and honey (see basic mead-with-grain recipe below).

Metheglins usually form cloudy brews that take a long time to clear – and may never do so. If you really do like your brews to be clear then you may have to add finings to the demijohn a few weeks before bottling. Expect to keep them for at least a year after bottling before the flavours have reached anything like their optimum.

I rarely brew metheglins. If I want mead to taste of spices then I will 'mull' ordinary mead or melomel (see recipe below) with spices and fruit just before serving. Served warm it makes an excellent wintertime drink and one especially suitable for Yuletide celebrations.

Basic cyser recipe

Unless you are a beekeeper then the amount of honey needed for basic mead makes it rather expensive. However by adding apple or grape juice a cheaper – and more traditional – type of mead can be brewed.

For one gallon of cyser:

> one pound of honey
>
> two cartons of apple juice (preferably the type sold refrigerated rather than the 'long life' varieties)
>
> one sachet of white wine yeast

Dissolve the honey in a saucepan of warm water (as described above). Pour into the demijohn, add the apple juice and the yeast then add enough lukewarm water to fill the demijohn to the shoulder. There's no need for yeast nutrient but apart from that everything else is the same as the basic mead recipe.

Cysers are usually more cloudy than other meads but that doesn't affect the taste!

Basic pyment recipe

For one gallon of pyment:

> one pound of honey
>
> *either* two cartons of grape juice (preferably the type sold refrigerated rather than the 'long life' varieties)
>
> *or* half the amount of grape concentrate needed for a demijohn of white wine
>
> one sachet of white wine yeast

As all homebrewing suppliers offer grape concentrates it is best to read the instructions that come with the concentrate but *halve* the quantities of grapes.

An indifferent brew of white wine can usefully be blended with a dry mead. Technically such blends of wine and mead are not pyments but instead are called **hippocras.** Traditional hippocrass recipes also include herbs considered to be beneficial to health. But whether or not hippocras was invented by the ancient Greek physician Hippocrates is a matter or debate!

Basic omphacomel recipe

I never call this omphacomel – to me it's just 'mead lemonade'!

> 2½ pounds (1.13 kg) of honey
>
> 1 sachet white wine yeast
>
> juice and pulp from six to eight large lemons

The trick is to get the right balance between the sharpness of the lemons and the sweetness of the honey. Frankly I'd recommend brewing some 'basic dry mead' at the same time so you can always blend some of this in at the bottling stage if the lemony taste is a bit too astringent!

I did try making gooseberry omphacomel once. But it tasted far too strongly of gooseberries and had to be blended with a lot of bland wine – I used up some rather tasteless parsip wine that way, then brewed some rice wine specially to mix with the rest of the gooseberry brew!

Other omphacomel recipes

If you've got a grapevine growing in your garden but the grapes fail to ripen then crush them and use instead of the lemons. Similarly for crab apples.

Unripe grapes and crab apples are best 'whizzed' in a food processor to break them down. Then put the 'mush' in a saucepan and bring briefly to the boil. This will kill off the wild yeasts which will otherwise give an unpleasant taste to the brew.

'Omphacomel champagne' recipe

Another excellent option is to start with only two pounds of honey then go for secondary fermentation in the bottle. See the recipe above for mead champagne for details.

One word of warning – it may taste like lemonade but do bear in mind it will likely be 8 to 12 percent alcohol. It's a great way to get squiffy rather too quickly! Announcing that 'ill-considered quaffing of omphacomel champagne is the cause of my consternation' is likely to prove difficult...

If you produce an omphacomel with the right balance between sharpness and sweetness then you've earned your stripes as a homebrewer. To get the balance right after secondary fermentation puts you in the 'master class'. Be happy if you get it about right the first few times – and congratulate yourself with a few more 'wassails' than usual if you think you've really hit the mark!

Basic melomel recipe

Mead made with naturally sweet fruit is called 'melomel'. Blackberries, blackcurrants, strawberries, raspberries and plums are all suitable and create distinctive meads. Mead made with mulberries is called 'morat' and mead made with rose hips is referred to as 'rhodomel'.

One gallon of melomel or morat or rhodomel requires:

> one-and-a-half pounds of honey
>
> one pound of fruit (in the case of plums add a little more because of the stones)
>
> one sachet of wine yeast.

Place the fruit in a saucepan and cover with water. Bring briefly to the boil. This will kill off unwanted wild yeasts. Usually it is sufficient to squidge the fruit with a potato-masher to make it small enough to funnel into the neck of a demijohn, although a food processor can be used if you prefer (except for plums or other fruit with large stones).

Dissolve the honey in warm water and add to the demijohn. Add the yeast then fill the demijohn to the shoulder with warm water.

Other people's recipes use more fruit. But this can lead to a fruit wine with a bit of a sweet honey taste. I prefer the mead to be the dominant flavour with just a pleasant fruitiness. This recipe should brew out quite dry. If towards the end of fermentation at the stage when you are ready to top up the liquid to the neck of the demijohn it tastes a little too dry then mix one or two dessertspoons of honey in with the warm water used for topping up. But don't be tempted to add any more than this!

To be honest, getting the balance right is tricky so my preferred way of making melomels is to blend a demijohn of fruit wine (made without any honey) with two demijohns of dry mead! Put this into carbonated drinks bottles and leave for a few weeks. It will almost certainly start secondary fermentation in the bottles and you have an deliciously effervescent drink. I would say it is best served chilled in summer but, because fruit ripens in the autumn and the brew is ready by early spring, I've yet to have much left by the summer!

Basic mead-with-grain recipe

Interestingly, although there are special names for meads made with different types of fruit there is no established name for mead made with grains. I think this is because at one time *all* mead was made with grain (except for the more wine-like meads made from fruit which acquired distinctive names). Only when hops start to be added is there a special name: 'braggot' or 'brackett'.

Mead made with barley would be closer to ale than wine, doubly so if hops were also used. Before hops were commonplace in brewing then meadowsweet (*Filipendula ulmariai*) would have been used – this is why meadowsweet is also known as 'mead wort'.

The only grain-based wines I have brewed have simply used rice, white sugar, white wine yeast and yeast nutrient. This was blended specially to dilute some gooseberry omphacomel which tasted far too strongly of gooseberries! (I had previously diluted some of the gooseberry omphacomel with bland parsnip wine so knew that the bland rice wine was all that was needed.)

Substituting honey for white sugar gives the following recipe:

> one-and-a-half to two pounds of honey
> two pounds of brown rice
> one pound of raisins
> white wine yeast
> *either* one teaspoon of yeast nutrient
> *or* the juice of a large orange

Mince the raisins in a food processor then put with the rice in a saucepan. Cover with two to three pints of water and leave to soak overnight.

Note that I've never made this recipe with honey. Unless you are making it for blending (in which case why use honey, you might as well use the same amount of white sugar) then it needs meadowsweet or hops or something equally flavoursome to be worth drinking!

Much as I believe that mead was originally made with grains and meadowsweet I've never had a reason to 'experiment' with recipes and brews made this way. Similarly I have no experience of brewing beers and ales. The main difference of course is that wine yeasts produce at least eight percent alcohol whereas ales use different yeasts – brewers' yeasts – which will normally brew to between four and six percent. This in turn means that ales are drunk much younger than wines – indeed one of the challenges of home beer- and ale-making is for consumption to keep up with production!

But any recipe which uses barley and/or malted barley and hops could be adapted so honey replaces some of the grain. If you know where to pick meadowsweet then try substituting that for the hops.

Honeyjack

Mead can be distilled to a brandy or liqueur strength. Except it's illegal! And distillation is a tricky art which instead of concentrating the ethanol can easily distil serious toxins that cause severe headaches and even blindness.

If you really must flout the law then 'freeze distillation' is much safer. Place the mead in a freezer until it is slushy mixture. Crush the ice and strain the whole lot through a sieve. Keep the liquid and throw away the ice. This is sometimes called 'honeyjack' as this is the same way applejack is made from cider.

Other mead recipes

If you want to get totally perplexed then search the Internet for mead recipes! Hundreds of sites will offer their suggestions, although it is not always clear if these are 'tried and tested'. Many people seem to go for recipes with more ingredients than the basic ones I have listed here. But I strongly recommend trying out the basic ones first, then blending brews together at the bottling stage. No doubt you will form you own ideas about what works well – and what doesn't! That's why it is so important to keep your notebook up to date. If you keep detailed notes of each batch then it is possible to repeat your successes and learn from the less good batches.

The last drops

Even if you've no intention of brewing mead then I hope these recipes give some idea of the care and attention which goes into meadmaking. At least you will begin to understand that it's not the sort of drink which should be quaffed willy-nilly. As I say, 'You can't just drink it!'

If you're drinking someone else's brew then don't forget to include a heartfelt 'Wassail' to the mead-maker before any passes your lips.

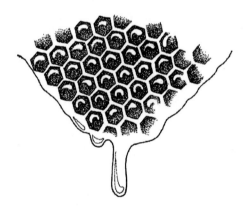

Sources

various Wikipedia pages, especially entries for mead; mead of poetry and Kvasir

anon, 2012, 'White House divulges Barack Obama's honey beer recipe', www.bbc.co.uk/news/world-us-canada-19454412

Beswick, Francis, 1994, *Traditional British Honey Drinks*, Heart of Albion.

Billington, Penny, 2011, *The Path of Druidry: Walking the Ancient Green Way*, Llewellyn.

Bray, Daniel, 1999, 'Sacral elements of Irish Kingship', in Carole M. Cusack and Peter Oldmeadow (eds), *This Immense Panorama: Studies in Honour of Eric John Sharpe*, School of Studies in Religion University of Sydney.

Enright, Michael J., 1996, *Lady with a Mead Cup: Ritual, prophecy, and lordship in the European warband from La Tène to the Viking Age*, Four Courts Press.

Glosecki, Stephen, 1989, *Shamanism and Old English Poetry*, Garland.

Kass, Sam, 2012, 'Ale to the Chief: White House beer recipe', www.whitehouse.gov/blog/2012/09/01/ale-chief-white-house-beer-recipe

Kloman, Harry, 2008, 'All About Tej'; online at www.pitt.edu/~kloman/tej.html

MacLellan, Gordon, 1996, 'Dancing on the edge: shamanism in modern Britain' in G. Harvey and C. Hardman (eds), *Paganism Today: Wiccans, Druids, the Goddess and ancient earth traditions for the twenty-first century*, Thorsons.

McGovern, P. E. *et al.*, 2004, 'Fermented beverages of pre- and proto-historic China', *Proceedings of the National Academy of Sciences* - Early Edition 101 (51): 17593–8.

Pollington, Stephen, 2009, *The Mead Hall: Feasting in Anglo-Saxon England*, Anglo-Saxon Books.

Tolley, Clive, 2009, Shamanism in Norse Myth and Magic (2 Vols), Academia Scientaum Fennica (Helsinki).

Trubshaw, Bob, 2012, *Souls, Spirits and Deities*, Heart of Albion; online at www.hoap.co.uk/general.htm#ssd

Heart of Albion's best selling title!

A User-Friendly Dictionary of Old English

5th edition with Old English reader

Bill Griffiths

This dictionary contains some 3,500 of the commonest words in Old English. Beginners will be able to translate simple passages of prose and verse from the rich variety of Old English texts. Advanced students will find it a rapid reference aid.

Words are listed by order of the consonants they contain, rather than by the usual strict alphabetical order of all letters in the word. The variation in Old English in stressed vowels at different times and in different dialects, plus many variants of spellings, can make it tricky to look up words in conventional Old English dictionaries as you are repeatedly referred to another entry. This problem is largely eliminated here and the user should find this dictionary offers an easy and speedy way to locate Old English words.

For the fifth edition the Introduction has been fully revised and a selection of representative Old English texts included. These will start you on the path of appreciating a very special literature and the way the language works.

ISBN 978 1872 883 854. 2005. A5, 108 + viii pages, paperback.. **£9.95**

'Highly recommended'
Folklore Society Katharine Briggs
Award 2003

Explore Folklore

Bob Trubshaw

**'A howling success, which plugs
a big and obvious gap'**

Professor Ronald Hutton

There have been fascinating developments in the study of folklore in the last twenty-or-so years, but few books about British folklore and folk customs reflect these exciting new approaches. As a result there is a huge gap between scholarly approaches to folklore studies and 'popular beliefs' about the character and history of British folklore. *Explore Folklore* is the first book to bridge that gap, and to show how much 'folklore' there is in modern day Britain.

Explore Folklore shows there is much more to folklore than morris dancing and fifty-something folksingers! The rituals of 'what we do on our holidays', funerals, stag nights and 'lingerie parties' are all full of 'unselfconscious' folk customs. Indeed, folklore is something that is integral to all our lives – it is so intrinsic we do not think of it as being 'folklore'.

Explore Folklore provides a lively introduction to the study of most genres of British folklore, presenting the more contentious and profound ideas in a readily accessible manner.

ISBN 1 872883 60 5. 2002. Demy 8vo (215x138 mm), 200 pages, illustrated, paperback **£9.95**

Heart of Albion

Publishing folklore, mythology and
local history since 1989

Further details of all Heart of Albion titles online at
www.hoap.co.uk

All titles available direct from Heart of Albion Press.

Please add £1.30 p&p (UK only; email
albion@indigogroup.co.uk for overseas postage).

To order books or request our current catalogue please contact

Heart of Albion Press
113 High Street, Avebury
Marlborough, SN8 1RF

Phone: 01672 539077

email: albion@indigogroup.co.uk
Web site: www.hoap.co.uk